Revel

Revel

Michael Indemaio

Acrylic Verbs Press
New York, New York

Acrylic Verbs Press
New York, New York

ISBN: 978-0-9713503-2-8

Library of Congress Control Number:
2016905684

Printed in the United States of America

Contents

1	Reduce Me
2	Caffeine & Anticipation
3	First Law of Attraction
4	If I Were the Wind
5	Directions
6	I Like to Catch You Staring
7	Truth in Letters
8	A Lot of Music
9	I Wish I Could Write You
10	Pizza
11	Ferocious Little Flower
12	Advice to a Younger Man
16	Eternal
17	How to Maximize Your Time
18	Mysterious Ways
19	Nothing Prepared Me for You
20	To Be Clear
21	The Universe Holds You
22	In Defense of Heartbreak
25	In Defense of Healing

27 In Defense of Whatever It Is
You're Feeling

28 Looking Back

31 Violence

32 No Such Things as A One-
Sided Wall

33 Let's Get Lost

34 Missing You in Dreams

35 I Want to be One of the Reasons

36 Happiness

37 To

38 I Write a Lot about the Weather

39 Loving You Is

40 The Remnants of Me

41 No Poetry as Deep as Your Eyes

42 A Poet with Nothing Else

43 Love Is I'm Sad

44 You on the Other Side of Rain

45 The Relativity

46 Paths

47 Parenthetically

48 Aesthetic #327

49 Cosmic Heart

50 3am Again

51 Promises and Fears

52 Good Teachers Give Art

53 Feelings this Heavy

54 Tell Me Everything

55 Tonight is as Dark as I Miss You

56 The Art of Letting Go

57 You're the One

58 Agape

59 Second Law of Attraction

60 Memories Are Best

61 Kill Me a Thousand Times

62 The Only Alternative

63 Dreams

64 Talking to Stars

65 When I Met Her She Told Me

72 Fight or Flight I've Got You

73 Favorite Artist

74 Cause and Affection

75 Maturity

76 The Symbiosis of Self-Reliance

77 Comfort and Warmth
78 Simple Things
79 Don't Go
80 History
81 Eating Light
82 Secret
83 You Have No Idea
84 My Awkward Means I Like You
85 My Happiness is Next to You
86 My Favorite Story of All Time
87 Things That Remind Me of You
88 Most Lessons Are People
89 Other People's Ghosts
90 I Hate When I'm Mad at You
91 I Believe in Us
92 Love Is a Choice
93 Suddenly the Sunrise
94 Louder
95 Horizon
96 A Mistake Not to Make
97 Muses and Moonbeams
98 Someplace Better

99 Revel
108 Talking to Stars
109 Still Life
110 Grounded and Exalted
111 Your Eyes like Clouds
112 It Only Takes Once
113 Remember That War We Won
114 True Story of a Tiny Hero
115 You on the Wind
116 Trust Me I've Imagined
117 The Story of Everything
118 First You're Okay
119 Never Stop Talking
120 I Am an Artist
121 A Question of Inspiration
122 Redefined
123 Reason
124 Executed
125 You Make Everything Crash
126 Sleepwalking
127 You Are so Many Colors
128 Edited

129   Method and Mindset

131   On Birthdays and Life

132   Quantum Heartstrings

133   Tulips on Fire

135   Aesthetic #482

136   Thanksgiving

137   Ice

138   I Don't Think You're Beautiful

139   Impossible Things

140   Candlelight

141   Prayer

142   Nocturne of a Restless Heart

143   Sacred

150   Love Is More Beautiful

151   I Can Love You from Anywhere

152   I'll Never Be the Same

153   Poetry Won't Do. I Need You.

154   The Girl of My Dreams?

155   I'm Sorry I Didn't Say Anything

156   Too Nice

157   To Get Out Alive

158   A Special Kind of Madness

160   Third Law of Attraction
161   I Miss You. How Dare You.
162   Jailbreak
163   I Didn't Feel Alone
164   If My Life Were a Christmas Movie
165   A Simple Request
166   Love Anyway
167   Heart-Shaped Paradox
168   Ontology
169   Talking to Stars
170   Falling Forever
171   Those Certain Days
172   I Remember the Moment
173   Sensitive
174   Wonder & Awe, Lost & Found
175   Miracles
176   Intervals
177   How Many Poems Have to Die
178   New York
179   What Healthy Love Looks Like
180   Leadership

181   Sticks and Stones Etcetera

182   Your Heart Is a Secret

183   Social Eyes

184   With Her it's All Music

185   Phantom Embrace

186   Scars are Strong

187   If I Could Have Coffee With
       You

188   Of All the Things Killing Me

189   You Light Beam

190   You Shining

191   A Very Short Love Letter

192   I Don't Know Anything

193   Somber Dreams For a Friend
       Who Couldn't Sleep

Preface

There are love poems everywhere.
You'll notice them in the eyes of young
couples (who don't notice anything but
each other's eyes) but also in the
knowing glances of older couples (who
know each other better than I know
anything). They are visible in parents
everywhere, and in those friends who
always seem to be there, wherever you
are. They can be found in heartbreak
and loneliness, and in perseverance
through pain.

Human life can be brutally hard, this is
undeniable. To an outside observer
(merely breathing but not quite alive)
it can seem a terrible burden. We all
know the pain is real, but is it the
point? I say no. I say it is the anagogic
understanding that touches the truth,

and for that we have to dive deep. We have to live fully and find the poetry.

I suppose I have a lot of thoughts about art and aesthetic, style and theory, and someday I'll probably express them. For now it seems enough to say that I am a real person. You can find me on social media and you can find me walking city streets in spring, observing the flowers and love poems.

This book is a collection of such poems. They exist because (contrary to the shouting of the unalive) pain and cruelty and death and war can not undo and will never silence love. Life is shockingly beautiful, and bursting with meaning. Don't watch it go by with disinterest and sorrow. There are love poems everywhere. Revel.

Revel

Reduce Me

Reduce me to a picture in a locket
to a love letter
you can fold
and fit inside your pocket,

reduce me
if you must
in order to keep me near...

Not fitting in your life
is still my biggest fear.

Caffeine and Anticipation

Your empty chair
      was screaming,

"Where is she, where is she?
 Why is she late?!"

I still get excited
and nervous—

every day, is our first date.

First Law of Attraction

Being yourself
isn't always
      the easiest way
to attract people,

but it's the only way
to attract people
who will love you.

If I Were the Wind

If I were the wind
                I would blow

the hair from your eyes

and if a speck of dust
                were to hurt you

I would die.

Directions

Asked a guy for directions
   he said "three blocks up
               make a right,"

but I could've sworn I heard,

"go to her and stay there,
  it's the only way to everywhere."

I Like to Catch You Staring

I like to catch you
              staring at nothing

smiling so slightly
even you don't know,
              and then

right before you fall
into sadness

              I like to catch you.

Truth in Letters

I write the truth in letters
that I know I'll never send,

sentences like stitches
for a heart that never mends.

I wish words and hope could heal me,
but my truth is not heroic…

I just want to be the secrets
you keep hidden in your notebook.

A Lot of Music Reminds Me of People but Only You Remind Me of Music

You are a love song
that my heart can't stop playing

and even the memory
of your melody
keeps my heart swaying.

I can hear you've been hurt,
but that's okay:

tell all of your demons I don't care,

I'm staying.

I Wish I Could Write You

I wish I could write you
a love poem

(silent
  breathless
  alarmed),

I wish I could write you
  (a love poem)

from my heart
into my arms.

Pizza

A few days after
you told me you loved me

mouth full, adorable
you said,

"Wow, I love pizza,"

and I assumed you meant
something different.

Ferocious Little Flower
You're the One

She's like a flower
in the middle
    of a warzone

if that flower
somehow

was winning the war.

Advice to a Younger Man
(You'll Find Her)

If I could reach back in time and talk
to myself, or if I had a son to teach
life's great lessons to, for the most part
I wouldn't know what to say. There's
no right way to live, no particular path
to follow — there is only being a good
person, and embracing love. Life is a
miracle to be spent in celebration and
awe, and it is more powerful and more
profound (more moving and beautiful
and unexpected) than anyone can ever
prepare you for. I would tell the young
man this one thing: you'll find her.
Plan on it.

She will be unexpected, arriving just as
you begin to stop believing in such
things. You will know as soon as you
see her, but you will not know her. She

will be so stunning that you will fall silent and stumbling at her glance, and you will think she is the most beautiful girl you've ever met, but you won't know why — not yet. You will have to speak to her, you will have to chase her. Never listen to the bitter old men who tell you to ignore her, and never listen to the voice inside (the little nagging self-hating voice) that says she won't want you. Be bold. Tell her. Don't waste time. Beg if you have to. Fight for her. Let the whole world see how you feel. Never look away, and never refuse her.

You will quickly learn who she is. Her personality will emerge colossal and clear and she will be unlike anyone, unlike anything you ever imagined — and she will undo everything you ever thought that you knew... She will have insecurities (because she will not really understand her beauty), and you will laugh at them. Yes, she will make you laugh — at everything, at nothing. She will challenge you, and redefine you, and you will not mind. You will see in her what others miss, and you will delight in how she responds whenever they underestimate her. You will guard her fiercely and you will prioritize everything in order behind her. You will find the world in her details. You will want to give her all that you have, and you should plan for that now, because you will want to have much to give.

If she has needs or desires that you cannot meet, you will hate yourself. If she is hurt by your mistakes and your failures, you will die. And yes... if she suspects in you a coldness, or if she fears your dark heart... if she senses in you an inability to love her... you will surely lose her. Then, nothing else will ever matter again. No accomplishment or acquisition will satisfy you, and the very taste of life will be pointlessness.

Do what you want with your life, and do what you're good at. Do what you enjoy. Follow your dreams, and work hard. Just know that she's coming.

You'll find her.

Eternal

Forever and Always
met for a drink

and
Forever said something

that made Always think:

"All that we are is pieces,
  with love as the link."

How to Maximize Your Time

Don't fall in love
with anyone
who won't be your best friend,

don't
listen, on life,
to those
who don't know death,

and never,
ever

hide your heart.

Mysterious Ways

They say things happen
for reasons,
but we don't
always see them.

I think I happened
to go through a lot,
to find you

right at this spot.

Nothing Prepared Me for You

I met you
as you met yourself

surprised by
all your depth.

I let you
as you let yourself

take away
my breath.

To Be Clear

By forever I mean
into the dark
beyond
                understanding

tomorrow
of all tomorrows

when all is said and done

and nothing remains
but our love.

The Universe Holds You

I screamed
   all my feelings

into the vast unknown
and you were its reply.

The universe holds you
in its every thought

and so do I.

In Defense of Heartbreak

I know there are a lot of people lining up to tell you it's okay when you know full well it isn't. They want you to know about the fish in the sea as if you aren't drowning.

They probably tell you about how the right one wouldn't leave you, as if they're not also saying you were wrong. They want you to not hurt because it wasn't really love. Except that it was.

That's the remarkable truth: you managed to love someone. And maybe they weren't worth it and maybe they didn't love you back and maybe even it didn't matter then and it still doesn't matter now. But your relentless heart loved, and now it hurts. Why wouldn't you collapse into the beauty and pain of it? Shouldn't a love lost be marked by tears? What kind of person do they think you are that you could be forced to put away your love and feel anything but utter sadness?

No, you are a bright and beautiful and profoundly decent person and you will feel the required and resulting feelings appropriately. You will feel them until they're done and you will take them with you and because it is the nature of heartbreak they will make you more beautiful still.

There is nothing I can say to make you feel better, but everything you feel is making you better all the time. You loved and now you're hurt and I can't think of anything more beautiful.

Pain is no reason not to love, and love
is the best reason for anything,
even pain.

In Defense of Healing

You don't owe anyone your suffering,
and your love has nothing to prove.

It's okay to let go
and it's okay to move on.
It's okay to carry with you
astronomical pain,
and still laugh everywhere you go.

Whatever hurt you
does not have to hurt you forever.

Your history hardly matters.
Those who know pain,

more than anyone,
deserve to know joy.

There is nothing lesser
in wanting better

and goodness demands a real strength.

It is not naïve to say
   you have seen both sides
      and are choosing the light.

It's okay
to be okay.

Here is my promise to you:
they will resent you for being well

and you won't mind.

In Defense of Whatever It Is You're Feeling

Feel whatever you feel
as long as it's real

you don't have to worry
about those who can't deal.

Looking Back

The heartbreaks grew in intensity
and absurdity,
          but were worth it
          and not just for the lessons.

I've never stopped loving anyone.

I try too hard to do right
when I should do smart—
or anyway that's what I'd say
          if I believed in that.

As a boy I watched another boy get
punched in the face again and again
for his non-violence,
          and it was the bravest thing
                    I'd ever seen.
I think of it often.

I am impractical in my DNA

and I am blessed.

I saw my grandparents when they were
still here and strong
and I remember my siblings as babies.
                I've had my heart broken
            by some of the greatest people
and
I've been moved to tears
        and not known why,
and I'd like to do that again someday
if I can find the time.

New York was my home and it was
beautiful and ruthless...

you can't help but to learn how evil
does its worst through good people.
It makes me laugh and it makes me
                                want to weep.

                Growing up was hard

and I'm terrified growing old
will be harder.

I've written thousands of poems
but I don't apologize for that.

I have seen angels
visit from Heaven
to hand me a flower
as if that was enough

and I've smiled and laughed and cried
because the way you get saved

is you get loved.

Violence

I've known a lot of violence,
the way anything wild does

but I've yet to see anyone
throw a punch

out of bravery.

No Such Thing as
A One-Sided Wall

Open your heart
not just to what wants in,

but also,
to what wants out.

Let's Get Lost
Like There's Something to Find

The way we bury ourselves
into books
I want to bury myself
in your eyes.

I want to look for that meaning
that fills a heart
like a mind.

Missing You in Dreams

Maybe I'll dream of you tonight
but it probably won't be right,

there will be some little detail
off, and on
           top of that

it will be too much
about my fear, and not enough
about you

who is my courage.

I Want to be One of the Reasons
You Keep Trying

You, hidden in shadows
where you go
to be sad

let me in.

I have candles
blankets and bottles.

I have space enough
to hide you in my heart.

Happiness

Happiness is not like art,
which I create
and then enjoy
forever.

It is more like coffee,
which I consume
and make more of
as needed.

To

No, my love

we do not belong to each other,
we simply belong together.

With, is what you mean
to say,
not to.

You don't belong

"to"

anyone.

I Write a Lot about the Weather and Whether or Not You'll Stay with Me Through the Storms

The raindrops hit

    like piano keys

and you are the chorus
the chords
the soaring vocals

and I stand

mesmerized, in awe,

soaked to my core.

Loving You Is
The most Significant Thing I do

When I say I love you,
it's not ephemeral
or descriptive,
but actually
redundant.

Not like saying
it's cold this winter,
but rather,
winter is cold.

The Remnants of Me,
Planning the Future of Us

I'm so cold
your warm touch
could shatter me
into a million

little
pieces,

each one
obsessed
with reassembling
to have you do it again.

No Poetry as Deep as Your Eyes

There isn't enough poetry
in the world,
and there never will be,

but when you laugh
you nod your head,

and that's enough
for me.

A Poet with Nothing Else Still Has Poetry

This is a poem
that you'll never read,
but that doesn't mean
it isn't true.

There's a lot about me
that you don't see,
written there
because of you.

Love Is I'm Sad

Love is: I'm sad
and I miss you
while you sleep

but
I don't wake you,
so you can rest.

The only thing
I want
is whatever is best

for you.

You on the Other Side of Rain

The rain on my window
obscures the view

the way the tears
in my heart
make it hard

to see
what to do

and I can't tell you how much

I'm falling for you.

The Relativity of Our Expanding Cosmic Hearts

Everyone was always saying
how they'd like to stay up late
and talk about the stars,
but I was always
sleepless and alone
contemplating space

and waiting to meet you.

Now, even more than the moon
you keep me in balance
and comfort
in the dark.

Maybe we're not made of stardust,
maybe the stars are made of us.

Paths

You say the best way
is to take the highway

but when you say best,
you just mean fastest.

I think the best way
is walking slowly

together.

Parenthetically

(Sometimes I tell her I love her
  and then she asks me why...

  is it okay if I tell her
  that ever since I met her

  I no longer want to die?)

Aesthetic #327

I like the line breaks
and spaces

in poetry,

like the moment
after you walk towards me,
right before you speak

when I can't breathe.

Cosmic Heart

My love is like a universe
expanding all the time

it has no ceiling,
             has no floor

when you think
you've hit its limit

I only love you more.

3am Again

In the middle of the night
your absence is more present

as if the silence
is a tangible alone

and your memories
are pillows

set in stone.

Promises and Fears

I will hold you
when you're hurting
for no matter how long

if you promise

once you're healed
I won't get up
to find you gone.

Good Teachers Give Art,
Great Teachers Give a Canvas

A professor once asked me
if I needed help

finding
myself.

I said
someone not being
where you expect them to be

does not mean they're lost.

Feelings This Heavy
Have to Sink This Deep

I can think of you
and stare peacefully
at the ocean
           for hours,

but when I look
into your eyes

I feel like I might drown.

Tell Me Everything

I like when you lean in
to tell me a secret

as if the world
might conspire

to pull us apart.

Tonight is as Dark as I Miss You

Tonight is as dark as I miss you
with stars
as bright as your eyes.

If tomorrow doesn't mean
I can kiss you,

then the sun
might as well never rise.

The Art of Letting Go

Don't hold on anymore,
we've held on too long.

Just let go,
I want you to go.

I want you to leave,
come back and see...

how I will always be right here.

You're the One that Makes me Run

Of everyone I've ever loved
you're the one that makes me run.

I race to your side
and then run and hide,
when I fear that
your feelings are done.

But here is my promise:
that I'll never tire,
never lose my desire,

like any big heart
I'm a fool, not a liar.

Away is the way that I'll never run...

I'll never hide from the truth,
and I know you're the one.

Agape

She writes her poems like cathedrals,
and my footsteps echo
down the halls.

I know
it's just a metaphor,

but I feel safe
behind those walls.

Second Law of Attraction

The loneliness of being true
to yourself

and not fitting in

isn't nearly as bad
          as being false

and realizing

no one
really knows you.

Memories Are Best
When We're Making Them

My poems
could describe you
from memory
with detail
you wouldn't believe

but I'm not trying
to capture you

I just don't want you
to leave.

Kill Me a Thousand Times
I love You

The way you tap your feet
and tilt your head,
side to side
to the music.

As if it's involuntary.

As if you don't mean
to melt my heart.

The Only Alternative

If I can't be with you
I'll be alone

with the thought
of you,

and I won't notice
I'm alone,

won't stop thinking
until you're here.

Dreams

Your dreams may be too large
and too distant
to reach in one lifetime

but we can stay here
in love

and watch them
like stars

all at once.

Talking to Stars

Me:
I don't want to lose her.

Stars:
but she isn't here for you.

Me:
she isn't here for you either.

Stars:
ah, but we are here for her.

When I met Her
She Told Me of Heartbreak

When I met her
            she told me of heartbreak,

she opened up right away
and not because she was trusting
but because she could see
   something I didn't realize was in me.

The world had already hurt her
more than she could have imagined
and although she still believed in God
     she no longer believed in chance,

she said whenever something good
                     happens
she begins to wait for something bad.

She inspired the most selfless sadness
my heart had ever had.

She told me about
        the death of her mother
the way you might casually mention
the world is ending,

the way you might tell a group
                        of children
that there is no Santa, and that
the vast majority of them will give up
                        on their dreams
before they graduate high school.

She told me about friends who had
abandoned her and about bullies and
misfortunes and about the fear of
what would come next.

I'd interject softly with stories
about violence and death.

        —But mostly we laughed.

The sound of her voice
was worth more
than for which my heart ever asked.

After our first date
she began to wonder
what karmic price she would pay
        for our happiness.

I told her she was wrong
and silently noted
that she showed up
        for the second date anyway.

Since then, she has never
not showed up

and my heart has never failed
to applaud and erupt.

And yes, life sure keeps coming.

Art doesn't pay the bills
    and as much as it helps,
    love doesn't cure the ill.

The world is so ugly that when you
turn on the news you can't even find
the coverage of genocide between all
the discussions of which politicians
won't admit that they lied.

And when I go to work I come home
                      and bemoan
that once they sense weakness
the vultures won't leave you alone.
            I shut myself down,
        and silence the phone

            and I silence my fear

because although everything is cold
and unfair
    I get to tell her all about it

as I run my fingers through her hair.

And most of the time
we're laughing.

I can't stress that enough.

The day I met her is the day my life
became full of laughter and love…

and eventually
one of us will die
leaving the other one alone
and I just hope that she knows

death is the cost we will pay

nothing else.

Along the long way
we are reversing the curse:
it doesn't matter,

let life do its worst,
we will always be laughing even louder
than it hurts

and if there is a price for this
and the Lord decides He should take it
please
let me be the one who should pay it.

I know there will be no end
to the struggles and tragedies
but I also know
she will be there.

She will kiss me
until we're cured of society

and I will go forward
with love in my heart

and laughter beside me.

When I met her
　　　　she told me of heartbreak

　　and she was the most beautiful
　　broken thing
　　　　　I'd ever seen.

—Life is not defined
by the losses through time

but by the love that you hold
in-between.

Fight or Flight I've Got You

If you decide you must hide

I and my life will hold you
closer than close
deeper than deep

my black hole heart

will keep you safe.

Favorite Artist

I know someone who loves
the way I write.

I mean she loves
with rhythmic
stuttered
enthusiastic joy

and I want to be
her poetry

and light.

Cause and Affection

I like myself
when I'm with you,

when everything about me
is actually yours

as if I'm part of your beauty,
an effect of your cause.

Maturity

Age
does not give you wisdom

it gives you perspective,

(so does youth).

My maturity is this:

I am no longer afraid

to fall

asleep,
apart,
or in love.

The Symbiosis of Self-Reliance and Compassion

Teach yourself
how you don't actually need anyone

and you will gradually learn
not to take for granted

those who choose you in their life.

Comfort and Warmth

My life was uncomfortable
until I met you,
and decided to make your life ours.

Kind of like what you've done
with all of my hoodies.

Simple Things

All I want

        is proof

that someone else feels
all the things I feel

and then maybe
we'll listen to music.

Don't Go

Please don't leave me here
inspired and alone,

sleeping in my house
and dreaming of your love,

which is my home.

History

Human beings emerged and
                                    invented fire,

Christ rose from the dead,

and Shakesepare wrote a bit.

We had some wars and then
I kissed you.

Eating Light

You said you ate light today
and misunderstanding

I imagined you
devouring illumination.

All that radiance
which is, next to you,

                    a shadow.

Secret:

I don't care (not even a little)
about your new shoes,

but nothing
could be more important

than the way they make you smile.

You Have No Idea How Beautiful You Are Which Is Just One of Many Beautiful Things about You

You wear your modesty
                    like flowers

and I let you think it matters.

No one sees the flowers
when you walk into the room.

My Awkward Means I Like You

I have seen the tides rise
   at the sight of your eyes.

The world sways melodically
and looks at me smirking.

Then we laugh
and bow our heads.

My Happiness is Next to You

There's nothing I want to do
that wouldn't be better
    if we did it together.

Let's sit and talk
metaphorically
about the weather.

Just before we met
was the coldest winter ever.

My Favorite Story of All Time

My favorite story of all time is this: A girl and a boy lived in a magical land where they had many adventures and where they had to fight many enemies and sometimes the evil and beauty got too much and made them sad. Then they met each other and they had fun and made each other smile and laugh along the way.

After that it didn't matter how it ended because it was already worth it, and the real story was them.

Things That Remind Me of You

Joy, sadness, weather,
places, people, music,
message notifications,
and anything blooming quietly

                    like hope.

Most Lessons Are People

Everyone like me
                needs someone like you
to teach them a lesson
in humility.

You were like a secret
hidden deep within me,

I had to discover you
to cure my instability.

Other People's Ghosts
Are Real Enough

One of many ways I care for you:

People hurt you
    years ago

and I fight them every day.

I hate when I'm Mad at You
And You're Beautiful

You are in my head
                    please stop screaming,
everything you do seems so loud.

You are in my life
                    please don't leave me.

You are so deep a part of my every day
it would be years
before I could let you go, you,

you are in my heart, don't be reckless.

Don't be careless with what's there.

You are my everything, my everywhere,
show me how to show you
how I care.

I Believe in Us
More than You're Scared

Does it really matter
that we make mistakes every day,
                    or that
I can't give you
everything you deserve
or understand you
entirely when you're hurt?

Isn't that what love is for?

Doesn't love overcome
everything that keeps us apart, and
                    isn't it a lack of love
                that creates separation?

Let's call in sick and say it's our hearts.

I think we can make something perfect
from our shared imperfections.

Love Is a Choice

In a forest
of poet
trees
I'm
the one

you carved your name on.

Suddenly the Sunrise

When you can't see
any good on the horizon

remember
                    how few good things

ever announce their arrival.

Louder

I won't feel quietly,
my heart was not meant
        for delicate society.

I will scream and I will cry—
I will laugh and dance and fight.
I will react to you a million ways,
    but always with delight.

My voice has been perfectly designed
                to speak to you all night,
and when you don't want to hear
how I love you anymore
I will pick up a pen, and I will write.

I don't want you to ever have to
        question my affection,

let's make love our destination,
our journey, and our direction.

Horizon

Her eyes on
the horizon,

it reminds them
of beyond.

His eyes on her eyes on
the horizon,

and on and on
they go.

A Mistake Not to Make

To call infatuation love is an error.

To call love infatuation,
is blasphemy.

Muses and Moonbeams

My art is like the moon,
if you didn't know better

you'd think the light
                    was mine.

Someplace Better

I want to disappear deeply
into our secrets
until like magic

we arrive

together
at that place (together),

where the sadness can't find us.

Revel

Before I met you
        the oceans were just water
        and the stars didn't shine.

I marvel at the God who made you—
who gave me everything, and so
                taught me
      that nothing is mine.

Ownership is illusory
and we have nothing to sell
but our souls.

First there was the café with the
couches and then the place with the
tiny tables and the candle light and
somewhere in there was the park at the
center of the world — our spots, and I
felt at home there every bit as much as
at our home, which is to say, our place,

with the hard wood floors and monthly payments. It's all the same. They could have been anywhere.

Do you ever wonder what it all means?

Well, I wonder that it does.
It's amazing.

Does everything have meaning?

It does if we want it to.

There was that piano ballad that moved us and the pop song that made us move and also the oldie we both discovered we loved and the acoustic one with the words about us, and they were all our song... and that time we stayed up late in the rain, and that was our song too.

If you've ever left home

feeling like you've forgotten
something important,

that's what my entire life was like
before I found you.

> *When we met did you recognize me*
> *for who I would become?*

For who you've always been.

What would you do
if you lost me?

Tell me — what should I do?

Look for yourself I guess.
That's where I'll be.

They say pairs of quantum particles,
when separated, still behave in relation
to each other, no matter the distance.

You may not believe this, but I can feel
your heart rate change

from miles away.
I know you feel

three things
at once
and

sometimes in the middle of the day
in the middle of sunshine
and sentences
you cry and think no one notices
but I promise you I do.

The flowers began to bend and frost
shot up through the ground — ice was
everywhere charging towards everything
swallowing the city, and I gripped your
hand. The ice grabbed you at the ankle
and it tried to rise up your legs and
consume you and I just knew it wanted
your heart and I kissed you...

Explosions. The air was overwhelmed
with meaning and warmth as we walked
through the desolate cosmic city streets
and you said, "this...

> this is a nice night."

Is this a poem about me?

Yes, all of this.
It can't be any other way.

And yet there was a time...
a time before.

> No,
I think they've always been about you.
Even when I didn't know...

they were all about me,
and I am all about you.

Every word and every note and even every little moment in every dimly lit corner of existence.

Miracles, all of it.

And someday, you'll say
"I don't like it here, let's go,"
and we'll both go somewhere else.

Just like that.

I just want to be happy, all the time.
Sometimes I don't understand
why I'm not.

Maybe because
everything matters.
Maybe because you know some things
are worth mourning and everything is
worth feeling and nothing is empty or
meaningless. Maybe because you have
the best heart I've ever known.

There was that old place where the tear soaked walls made the piano keys sound as if surrounded by cotton and the red wine goblets would all harmonize with everything we tried to say. At the end we got up and walked out together — we didn't know where we were going and we walked out to the water. There was a sailboat, as if it had been waiting, and just us two, we sailed away. Deeper and deeper we went into the vast and big of the ocean until there was nothing else. The fog swept in and soon enough we were sailing on clouds... Mighty winds howled like the loud rolling laughter of angels, and everything began to shine with the light of a thousand stars. By that we could navigate — on something steady and true. The unwavering light.

When we arrive at that place
where God has been waiting

perhaps He will tell us we're home.

If for some reason, however
He asks where we'd like to be,
I will smile and tell Him "anywhere,"

and I know
He won't send me anywhere
                    without you.

And I know... you get sad...
                It's hard not to.
I know,
we seem so small
in the face of these miracles,
                    and yet,
                we are these miracles.

We will always have each other's hearts
    the way the birds have the sky.

                    You and I, I think

we will always be together.

I think we always have been.

Even when I'm sad, I'm in love.

Talking to Stars

Me:
I tried to tell her how I feel…

Stars:
tried to?

Me:
I did the best I could.

Stars:
if you used words,
that wasn't your best.

Still Life

Roses in wine bottles,

(memorials
      to your delicate
      fragility
 so wild and refined,
 exceedingly both beautiful
       and intoxicating)

     on my mind.

Grounded and Exalted

I want the truth to hold me
like the soil holds the roots,

and then I want to hold you
the way a prophet holds the truth.

Your Eyes Like Clouds
Build Up and Let Go

I wonder if
when raindrops

      drop

from the beautiful sky

they are aiming for you

to be home

   in your

      eyes.

It Only Takes Once

Once I saw your eyes
light with delight

I began to memorize
        everything you like.

How could anyone
            once
        having heard you laugh

not want to be very

                    very funny?

Remember That War We Won
by Walking Away Hand in Hand?

Here's the thing
about the high road:

It offers tactical advantage,
and the view is better.

True Story of a Tiny Hero

The bravest bird
flew off first
found her way
and made it safe.

She sings in peace
in paradise

and dreams of the day
the flock may arrive.

You on the Wind

The autumn breeze
reminded me

of you in your faded old sweatshirt.

All those cradled dreams,
snug and peaceful,

folded neatly in my arms.

Trust Me I've Imagined
Everything Perfectly

My whole life) I've

practiced for your
                    sadness

to say
with confidence:

hold my hand,
don't let go,
it'll work it's
a good plan

(in your hands.

The Story of Everything

Death said to Love
"you know you'll never win"

but Love just kept on singing.

First You're Okay, and Then You're Amazing

How well you withstand
a broken heart,
determines
the path of your life.

We take more risks
those who know,
great pain

and how to survive.

Never Stop Talking

I want you
to tell me
how you feel

because
sometimes

all I feel
is alone.

I Am an Artist

I am the tears of my friends and they
are my laughter. I have grown but not
changed. I will always be different,
I was never the same.

I am old songs swelling in dusty rooms
late at night, I am the moonlight
through the blinds. I am a book's page
corner folded forever.

I am a light beam and I am alive.

I am a piano ballad whispering what's
to come; I am an artist.
I see things for the truth that can't be
seen, and I feel more than I know.

The best thing I ever made
was when I made you laugh.

A Question of Inspiration

"How do you think of poems?"

I don't think of poems at all.

"What do you mean?"

I mean love.

"So you think of love?"

I think of her.

Redefined

I thought I was in love
the moment we met

but every day since
you have redefined
      the word,

bringing it to life
with meaning

and depth.

Reason

You are my reason
when I'm unreasonable

and my meaning
all day long.

Not easy, like
        "oh I could die for you,"

but better,

like really live.

Executed

It kills me how much
our love has become

something I need.

Our goodbyes are like guillotines,
I lose my head

when you leave.

You Make Everything Crash down around Me and It's Beautiful

When the stars began
to fall from the sky

no one on Earth
understood why

but the angels in Heaven
were preaching on high

about the gravity of love
and the look in your eyes.

Sleepwalking

We were both sleepwalking
when we left
from opposite ends
of the Earth

and we met in the middle
of the night

and slow danced till morning.

You Are so Many Colors and I Want to Paint with Them All

I don't mind
when you're too much,

because everything else
is never enough.

Edited

At first this was
a ten page poem.

(I've been editing
for days).

What's left
is this:

love and fear
are opposites

and you make me unafraid.

Method and Mindset for an Aspiring Poet

1. Be stubborn in love.
2. Take in influence like a child runs in play.
3. Individuality, not individualism.
4. A charitable spirit makes everything grow.
5. You'll never know a flower if you're set on hating gardens.
6. Symbolism is the language of the sacred.
7. Poetic means an elegant approximation of the ineffable.
8. Shame is not poetic, neither is hate.
9. Know which poets you love and why.
10. Your mind remembers more than you realize.
11. Write in your sleep.
12. You are never not a poet.
13. Sometimes don't write, but watch.

14. Never choose safe over inspired.
15. The most beautiful draft is best.
16. Poetry only shines if it's true.
17. Art is immeasurable,
    go to immeasurable lengths.
18. Poetry should flow like water
    but burn like fire.
19. Don't aspire when you can be.
20. Your heart travels joyfully
    surrounded by a poet.

On Birthdays and Life

Most of the time
I make healthy choices
      because I know
      life is precious.

Sometimes
I eat a bunch of cake,

for the same reason.

Quantum Heartstrings

Like how unpredictable
particles form objects
bound by classical
determinism,

I am composed
of a billion wild feelings
    that lead me to love.

Tulips on Fire

You said you were leaving,
                          Armageddon
in my heart
              you said

you didn't think we could work this out

as if I'd never brought you flowers
as if
          an infinity of colors
          don't dance on the light

you said you were sad,
and I can understand,
                              but love

remember we sat side by side
and it was as if the world
was building around us

and we can still tell it what to become.

Please don't make
the biggest mistake
                    of my life.

Everything is as possible
as you love me.

Aesthetic #482

Like the crack in the voice
   of your favorite singer

       and the creases
       in your notebook
       in your boots
       in your soul

like that crooked smile
   and wicked humor

like life and love and
so many things difficult but worth it...

it doesn't have to be

       flawless

   to be perfect.

Thanksgiving

With the hundredth psalm
tucked in my pocket
and nowhere else
to be

eyes to the sky
a satisfied smile;

I am happy, I am healthy
I am free.

Ice

Watching the melting ice
    I think of us

and how we were
in the beginning.

How you'd breathe on me,
and all I had become

would be undone.

I Don't Think You're Beautiful, You Are and I Notice

You were standing there
so casually

         and I thought
         how

strange it is
that people like you
are that beautiful

all day long.

Impossible Things

You changed my heart
     my heart changed my mind
     my mind changed my life

     and

like many impossible things
we happened.

We sat together, in silence,
as if nothing else mattered,

as if
     a universe had exploded
     into existence

thirteen billion years ago,

and we found love.

Candlelight

Your love is the part
of the candle flame
that sublimely
      lights up the room.

Mine is the steadier
base of the flame,
  unflinching,

  solid and blue.

Prayer

God please keep moving us
toward what you know
we need

and away from the suffering
of what we think
we want.

Nocturne of a Restless Heart

The moon melts
and dampens the night,

and while you sleep
burning brilliant and bright,

I gasp for your beauty,
I choke on the light.

Sacred

Modern thinkers take note:
a useful methodology
                    is not a substitute
for a sound philosophy,
and morality
is the most mysterious,
yet fundamental
component of wisdom.

A definition:

Sacred (*adjective*)
unassailable, inviolable
highly valued and important,
entitled to reverence and respect.

For example,
a rose can be sacred,
depending on why you take it.

I have been too much in love
                    to write love poems,
(to craft the words I want to scream
or subject the world
to my stuttered dreams),

but there are things that I just can't say
                                    to her.
I come close but then I retreat
fearful of my ugliness,
                    of my inadequacy.

See I remember being threatened
on rooftops and beaten in basements,
(I knew the addicts upstairs
and the drunks on the floor)
and I have grown into a poet, obsessed
with questions of intention
and seeking answers in that bottomless
rock bottom
that can be a bottle of whiskey.

I have seen the oncoming trains
        and like a compulsion,
a thought so depraved I stand beside it
in horror even as I think it, I think
how in an instant
the answers could be rendered

                                meaningless.
Some things have their effect
for no reason.
                They are without purpose
                    and then they are gone,
and after the chaos
everything beautiful dies.

Anyway, I can't tell her this.
I can't break this bad news about the
gravity of bottomless questions, dead
roses in inkwells and the scratching of
the pen's seething searching torture as
it seeks that next saccharine chorus but
keeps running up against an epitaph.

Here lies a failure, a poet as noted
who never understood what he meant
when he wrote it,
that death
is the disease, and the cure
for the hopeless.

I think of childhood,
and of my grandmother's

                    chicken soup,

and how no matter how much money I
spend on self-indulgence and blankets
I can't get back to that comfort...

and if I couldn't find it I used to fake it
and if I couldn't buy it I used to take it
and I learnt from modern thinkers
that if you can't have something
then you might as well break it,

but I never felt right in that immorality

146

and the greatest answer
that ever did come to me
is exactly what I can't tell her.

How

it might take a million people
to make you feel small and alone,

but it might take just one
to help you to grow…

and every miracle I've ever witnessed
has been trumpeted by her laughter

and when we're not speaking,
I'm thinking
of what to say,
and when she's not there
I don't feel like I'm anywhere…

and it may take a million questions
to find just one, really beautiful

answer.

Namely

how the healing of love
utterly transcends

the damage of hatred

and when she's in my life
even the pain becomes sacred.

Here lies a failure, a poet, a man
who wrote down a million questions
that he didn't understand,

but then put down his pen
to hold his love's hand.

Modern thinkers take note:
I don't care what I wrote.

My healing heart,
is just where the ghost of pain haunts.

Everything is sacred,
take the words you want.

Love Is More Beautiful than Romance May Seem

If I do it right, my love,
you'll never understand
my love,

as well as it understands you.

I Can Love You from Anywhere

It's not the distance,
but what separates us—
          that's the issue.

Invisibly you've been with me
and the next time I throw
                    caution to the wind,

I won't miss you.

First I'll conquer the world,
          in some metaphorical way

and then I'll kiss you.

I'll Never Be the Same

Since you left
I sleep

on your side of the bed,

feeling like it's me
who has disappeared.

Poetry Won't Do. I Need You.

I can't stop thinking of things
to say to you

which means when I see you
I will fall silent
and stare.

I get sad for no reason,
just remind me you care.

The Girl of My Dreams?

"The girl of my dreams,"
sounds like someone I'd leave.

I like that you're real.

I like that you're something

I never

>   could have
>   imagined.

I'm Sorry I didn't Say Anything

Sometimes
beautiful things make me quiet

and I hope they know
that's why.

Too Nice

Don't say your problem is
you're "too nice."

Maybe you're too passive,
but not too nice.

Niceness isn't a problem.

To Get Out Alive

Grow up fast
but grow old slow

know what you believe in
and believe in what you know.

If you listen to your heart
you'll know where to go.

A Special Kind of Madness

Love is a special kind of madness,

it overwhelms your reason
and supersedes your senses.

The heart is the place
                    where love is created,
it decides how much to make
and where you should place it.
It will grow as big as it must
to hold and contain it;

Hearts only break from the outside.

Once broken
a heart doesn't function the same.
Love begins to pour through the cracks
and leaking all over everything,
it can drive you insane.

In this vulnerable state
the heart will need outside protection,
encouragement, bandages,
and for the love, a direction.

But the good news is this:
Hearts only heal from the inside.

Love is a special kind of madness.

When properly handled
it can heal any wound,
and cure any sadness.

Third Law of Attraction

If they want you
before they know you,
it isn't you
they really want.

Your beauty
is the poetry,

what you look like
is just the font.

I Miss You. How Dare You.

For you I pull myself up
every morning, force myself
to sleep every night, and
in between
hold together a universe
of swirling chaos inside.

I don't mind,
just don't ask me to love you any less.

Come back to my heart,
because only you

can help me clean up this mess.

Jailbreak

Please let me rescue you
    if just for today.

If you decide
you don't like it,
we can go back to your prison
and patiently wait.

I Didn't Feel Alone until I'd Met
Thousands of People

The unappreciative will by their nature
consume your life
until there is no room left
for the type of people
        who would treat you right.

Take control of your life
or stop calling it yours.

The fear of being alone will lead you
to those who will make you feel lonely.

Fight that fear with faith,
and begin to build a miracle.

Live an extraordinary life
and extraordinary people will find you.

If My Life Were a Christmas Movie My Love for You Would Be the Snow

It's December again
I remember again
all those years that froze my poor heart

(please, sit by the fire with me,

 please
 warm me and then never leave).

A Simple Request

If you're going to love me
please love me completely,

don't forget the parts of me

that are stupid
and lonely.

Love Anyway

The bigger the heart
the more it will break.

The more that you offer,
the more they will take.

It's okay.

Love is never a mistake.

Heart-shaped Paradox

Strangely

an empty heart
has no room
            for anyone

while

a full heart
embraces the world.

Ontology

My cells replace themselves
and my body is renewed
every few years—

the soul is the thing that remains,
is unchanged,

dreams of you.

Talking to Stars

Stars:
heard you met someone beautiful...

Me:
yeah.

Stars:
what's she like?

Me:
kind of like you...
maybe a little brighter.

Falling Forever
Would Feel a Lot like Flying

I fall for you:
always.

It's never come and go
or ebb and flow

and never an end
but a deeper begin.

I always fall further.
I only fall in.

Those Certain Days

You are mine and I am yours,
and so we smile
just because
the birds in trees
the summer breeze
and our full hearts
sing as they please.

I Remember the Moment Our Eyes Met and I Wanted to Know How You Felt about Everything

I said hi like I knew you
because I no longer knew anything else

—when you picked up my heart
were you surprised how it felt?

All my sunsets and roses
    at your feet where they fell,
all your tears in my eyes as the tides
start to swell,

and I rise
to the heights you devise for me,

and I sleep in the depths of the sky.

Yes is the shape of my love for you,
and now is the color and size.

Sensitive

We agree
I am sensitive,
but you mean like a bruise

while a delicate scale
inside my heart
moves.

Wonder & Awe, Lost & Found

As a child I was taught
to break down the world
until I understood it.

Now I am rebuilding
the incomprehensible miracle
it really is.

Miracles

I believe in ghosts
      because I've been one...

      I believe in angels
      because I've kissed one...

and if you don't believe in miracles,

      it's because you've never had to
      miss one.

Intervals

The stars we see
are so far away
the light has travelled
here for years,

maybe
when I look at you
I am seeing a love

from the beginning
of time.

How Many Poems Have to Die Before We Sort This All Out?

I know someone
        who smiles like the sun

moves like a river,
and stares like a gun—

a beauty that tells you
there is nowhere to run.

She is threatening, and thrilling,

and something in her eyes
looks at me

as if we've barely begun.

New York

I want to send a love letter
to New York
and let it speak for me
until I get home,

where in a city of 8 million
you and I
will be alone.

Maybe This Is What Healthy Love Looks Like

Your strength doesn't scare me
and I don't need you
to need me,

but if you want me
I'll be there,

and if you love me
I won't leave.

Leadership

Bosses pay people
and demand obedience.

Leaders motivate people
and inspire allegiance.

Sticks and Stones Etcetera

Let's stop teaching kids
that words will never hurt them.

Words hurt,
and if you throw them at someone
it can take them
a long time
to heal.

Your Heart Is a Secret
I Would Keep

Kisses are like poetry,
their beauty
     depends on what they mean.

They are symbols,
               like roses and death,
which is to say
     you take away my breath.

There is no dark part of you
I would love any less.

—Please explain your heart to me,
  don't make me guess.

Social Eyes

Because you can't reach,
you hand me your drink,
to place on the table.

I do so happily

knowing just how many things in life
I can't reach without you.

Everyone in the room
can tell we're together, and
for years before I met you

they could see you in my eyes.

You, sitting there
silencing the universe.

With Her it's All Music
Without Her it's Sound

My
        baby,
                grand,

she sleeps silent
on my shoulder

        all her songs
still playing
in my head;

        our fingers locked
on the keys to everything

                to everything

writing a lullaby
about paradise
from a comfortable bed.

Phantom Embrace

You hold them and hold them
and hold them
until you're so used
to holding them

you feel them

when they're gone.

Scars are Strong

Do you get the feeling, it bothers them
how your heart grows

                            stronger
every time it breaks?

It's as if they want you to grow harder
without growing tougher,
but you always do the opposite.

I think we are on the right side
of a metaphysical dispute,

in which vulnerability is virtue
and love is the truth.

If I Could Have Coffee with You Every Morning, I Would Never Oversleep

Mornings now remind me
of you and your smile

as if I'd never had one before,

as if I was asleep
until we met and

coffee never woke me
until I shared it with you.

Of All the Things Killing Me
I Like You the Best

I told you I was emotionally
                           invincible

but the word
I was looking for

was indestructible.

You Light Beam

You light beam, you shining

you

enlighten me,
        when I feel dark.

You turn this merely poet
into poetry
                My Heart.

When
I reflect on you

    you reflect off me

and I think

you are the brightest thing
I have ever seen.

You Shining

I want to know how it is, you brighten,
                    not just the cloudy,

but the sunniest of days.

I hear the sound of light
                    in your laughter
and your words continue to glow
when you leave.

There's a light in your eyes
and in your smile.

Your hair is made of light
and your fingers
and your voice.

                    All you do is shine.

A Very Short Love Letter

You terrify me
and for the first time

I'm sure that's appropriate.

I Don't Know Anything
But This Feeling

I don't know about love
at first sight,
but I know I loved you quickly,
even though it took me years
to love myself.

Maybe opposites attract,
and maybe they don't,
but I know when you're sad
I want to be strong,
and when the world makes me cold
you feel warm.

I don't know what a soul mate is,
but I know I've felt alone
every second of my life,
except when you were there.

Somber Dreams
For a Friend Who Couldn't Sleep

Will power

is predicated on passion.

It comes through on intention
the way addiction regiments
what was once a reckless search,
now just dead weight in weary arms.

You spoke to me in tender moments
of your abusive past
and of lovers who stole your identity

—Love thieves—

because you never did trust again,
and now you only find your voice
through a completely
broken down will.

You were conditioned to respond
to beatings and abuse.

Defiantly you began to relish
       the pop of flesh on flesh,
it reverberates more than any weapon
                 and sticks.
You began to understand
           that no weapon
hurts quite as much as another person
and how when a human being
screams in agony

it doesn't feel like desperation,
doesn't bellow from the diaphragm
but somewhere down by the intestines,
boiling bile,
         projectile pain,
it shoots out
scratching the throat like gravel.

And by the time you hit the floor,

you forget about purpose...
and though the floor hits back,
just as sure as a fist,
you are struck only
                    by how hard you are;

because the pain is your own.
You own it, in completeness.

And there, in the pain,
                    you walk through dark alleys
                              on broken glass,

(because they don't clean those streets
too often)

and you stop to lift
half-burnt cigarettes off the ground,
your sensitive fingertips
                         scraping the floor
and then you light the cottony burn
of your death.

And it is a slow burn.
And it is a slow death.

And now you smell the smoke clearly
because you can't smell the air,
and if you stop and listen

                     you'll hear it,

the pop of flesh,
the agony of grown children,

screaming into pillows and
being beaten by parents
who live on that filthy street,

                     they live there.

And here's something else you won't
like listening to:

but I don't think you ever meant to
get drunk,

just sick,
and hungover.

It's like you don't really like being high
you just don't know how else to crash.

See,
you only ever fight for the beating.
But you don't have to accept it.

—And you don't have to accept it
because you don't have to accept it you
don't have to accept it you don't have
to accept it—

I woke you up that morning
after you finally collapsed,
and I picked you up off the street,

your words were dazed as they adjusted
to the light,
            and you didn't know who I was.

And then we sat there
for a few tender moments,

your soul sore and your skin hanging
lifeless off its skeletal frame,

and there I saw it in your eyes.

Make no mistake,
several times I have seen the fear
in your eyes

and if that makes you angry
then come at me,

but I won't fight back...
and I already forgive you.

Understand this:

When I left you I had nowhere to go,

and it was a beautiful spring day…

I found a place in the city where the
flowers grow wild, and that means
if you want you can pick one,
because they don't belong to anyone.

You see, it turns out
that you can be reckless in beauty
just as surely as you can be reckless

in pain

and there is no stain
that can't be washed clean,

no demon
that can't be sent home.

Just tell it to go.
        Tell them all, to go.

Because you don't have to accept it

and I have seen the smiles
of the recklessly beautiful
and they await you,
and they want nothing in return...

Will power
is predicated on passion.

You don't have to understand beauty,
you just have to want it.